Old BANBRIDGE

by

Alex F. Young, with photographs from the Des Quail col

The motorcade carrying Sir Edward Carson on his visit to Banbridge in 1913. Travelling with him were the Earl and Countess of Clanwilliam, Mr F.E. Smith and Captain and Mrs James Craig. After Banbridge they went on to Dromore where Carson laid the foundation stone of a new Orange hall.

First published in the United Kingdom, 2002,
reprinted 2008, 2010, 2011, 2013, 2014
by Stenlake Publishing Limited,
01290 551122, www.stenlake.co.uk

ISBN 9781840332049

THE PUBLISHERS REGRET THAT THEY CANNOT SUPPLY
COPIES OF ANY PICTURES FEATURED IN THIS BOOK.

FURTHER READING

The books listed below were used by the author during his research. None
of them are available from Stenlake Publishing. Those interested in finding
out more are advised to contact their local bookshop or reference library.
Capt. Richard Linn, *Banbridge*, Banbridge Chronicle Press, 1935.
Edenderry Primary School (ed. Doreen McBride), *Step Into the Past*,
    Adare Press, 1999.
C.E.B. Brett and Lady Dunleath, *Banbridge*, Ulster Architectural Heritage
    Society, 1969 and 1980.

ACKNOWLEDGEMENTS

The author wishes to thank Roy Martin, Mrs Iris Bramall, Andrew White,
Trevor Anderson, Joe Hozack, Steven Burgess, Rev. Norman Hutton, Alex
Curran, Gillian Close, Angela Dillon, Walter Porter, Roy Vogan, Plunkett
Campbell, Bertie Scappiaticci, James Vage, Robert Brown, Norman and
Ethel Murray of Fresh Winds, Jason Diamond and Banbridge Genealogy
Services, Paul McCandless and the Banbridge Orange Hall Committee,
Rita Harkin of the Ulster Architectural Heritage Society, and the libraries
at Banbridge, Armagh and Ballynahinch.

Left: An early twentieth century Fair Day, with cattle and haggling farmers
spilling out from the Cut onto Bridge Street and beyond. From the *Household
Almanac* we learn that fairs at Banbridge were held in January, June and
August, and there were also horse and cattle sales on the last Monday of
every month except August.

Opposite: Solitude House, seen here from the Water Bridge, was built in
1840 by the Clibborns, a Quaker family from West Meath, who established
a flour mill on the Castlewellan Road. The house found its solitude in
being on an island, flanked by the Bann and an early mill race which has
since been filled in.

INTRODUCTION

It was only in 1691, during the aftermath of the struggle between William III and James II, when an Outlawry Court sat in the town to deal with adherents to the latter, that Banbridge entered recorded history. Why it was chosen as a site for this court, in preference to Dromore, Loughbrickland or Lawrencetown, is unclear. In any case, the town's late start can be seen in its development as initially it was no more than a ribbon of houses along Bridge Street and Newry Street and not a more traditional community based around a market square. Late the town may have been, but it had two major advantages over its neighbours and was soon to eclipse all of them.

The town's coat of arms indicates its earliest industries by showing the River Bann (and the bridge which was built over it in 1832) with mussels which were once farmed in it, along with the shuttle and spindle of the cottage weaver. By the early nineteenth century the river was the first of Banbridge's advantages to take effect as it was powering a growing number of flax mills, and the second boost came in 1820 when the town became a staging post on the mail coach route between Dublin and Belfast. This contributed greatly to an improvement in the town's trading communications, although a few years later there was the threat of the town being by-passed by the route due to the difficulty in getting a coach and four up the two-way incline at the town's centre where the Bunch of Grapes Inn stood. This problem, however, was solved with a gift of £500 from the Marquis of Downshire towards the cost of the Cut, which allowed the roadway to be dropped some 15 feet and the predecessor of the Downshire Bridge to be built over it to link Scarva Street and Rathfriland Street.

By the early 1820s Banbridge's future was firmly invested in linen manufacture and the town was the centre of the 'Linen Homelands'. A contemporary writer noted, 'One of the best markets in this province, for the sale of fine lawns and linens, is held here. The town is provided with an excellent hotel [the Downshire Arms], a dispensary, a reading room and other useful public accommodation and on many accounts has a claim to eminent distinction in the history of Downshire.'

In 1859 pressure from the linen industry saw the opening of the railway line from Banbridge to Scarva. As the industry changed from water to steam power, the railway brought coal from the Newry canal, and, on return, carried the mills' finished products to world markets. Twenty years later the line was running to Ballyroney and Newcastle. The Banbridge to Belfast line, by way of Lisburn, Hillsborough and Dromore, opened in 1863.

Today, Banbridge stands as an example of how post-industrial towns can prosper. The linen industry has diminished, but is far from dead and the old skills are now employed in producing and hemstitching damask. Cotton and rayon are also now produced, along with linen thread, nylon filters for motor cars, clothing labels and ribbons. Diversity abounds; a factory on the Newry Road produces shoes.

The town's most famous son is Captain Francis Crozier, whose statue surveys the north-westerly horizon from his plinth in Church Square, but not far behind must come Joseph Scriven who penned the hymn, 'What a friend we have in Jesus'. Born in Seapatrick on 10 September 1819, his father was a captain in the Royal Marines. After two years at Trinity College, Dublin, he embarked on a military career himself, but poor health forced him to abandon this. On the day before his wedding, when he was about twenty-five years old, his fiancé was accidentally drowned. This, or the fact that his family were less than enamoured by his new found adherence to the Plymouth Brethren, saw him leave for Canada. The hymn, written about 1855 while he was at Port Hope, Ontario, was intended to help his mother at a time of sorrow. He died by drowning in Rice Lake, Ontario, on 10 October 1886. A memorial window to Scriven was unveiled at a dedication service in Seapatrick Parish Church, conducted by his great-great-nephew, the Right Rev. Henry Scriven, on 15 April 2002.

An early twentieth century view of Scarva Street, with Bridge Street running off to the right and Newry Street to the left, taken from the Downshire Bridge which was built in 1885. This was also known as Jingler's Bridge after the Lurgan apple seller who attracted custom by jingling coins in her pocket. On the left is the McClelland Memorial drinking fountain which was erected in 1906 to commemorate Dr Robert Brown McClelland, a local doctor. By 1965 it was considered a traffic hazard and was removed, firstly to Reilly Street and then to its present position at the Civic Buildings. Only after 1820, with the start of the Dublin to Belfast four-horse coach, did the steep incline of both Newry Street and Bridge Street towards this junction become a problem; this was solved by lowering the road and creating the world's first flyover with a bridge in 1834.

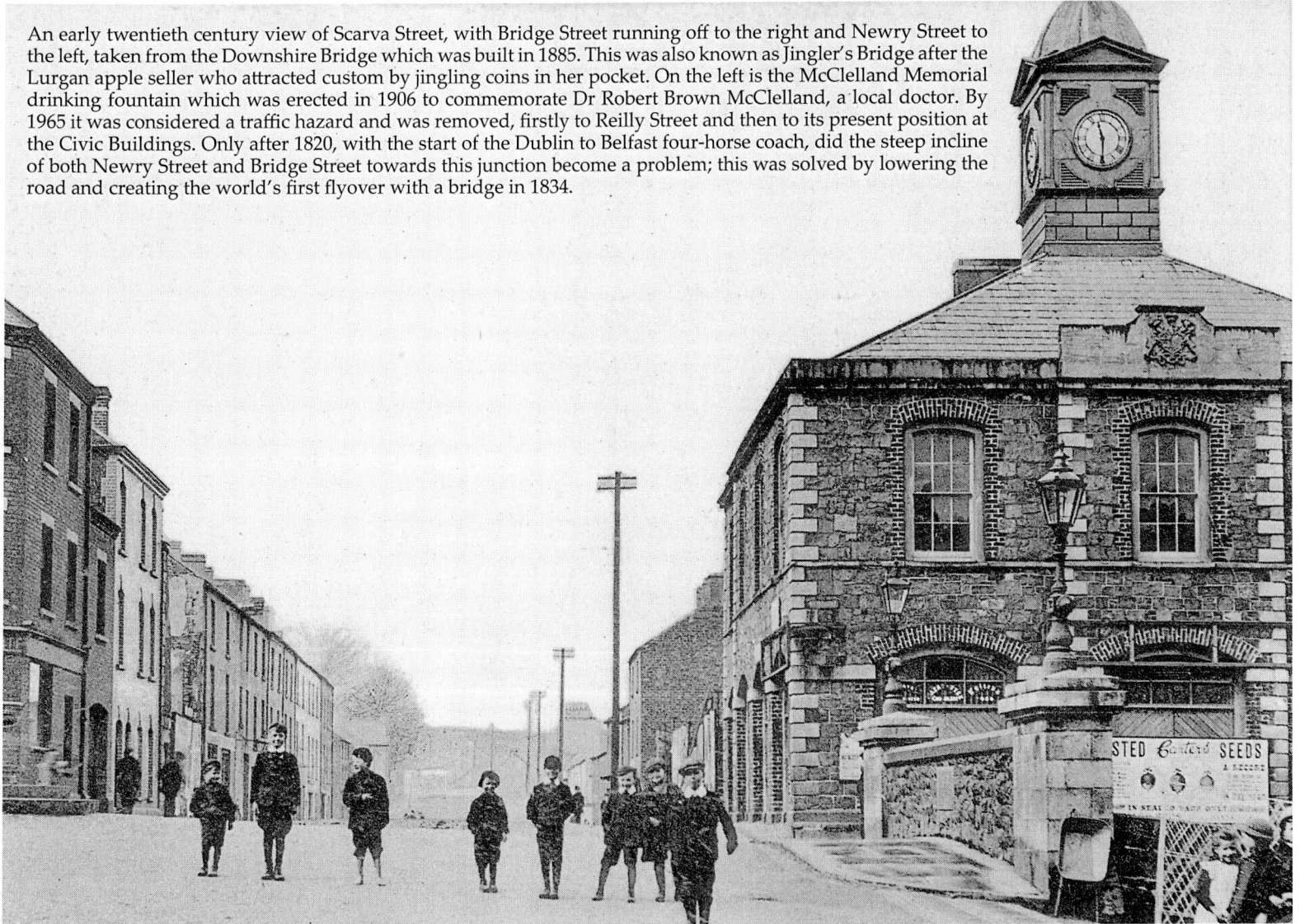

Newry Street on a summer's morning in 1910 as the horse-drawn van of McIlroy's Steam Bakery turns to continue its deliveries. From his premises in Rathfriland Street, McIlroy supplied 'Fancy Bread', a range of pastries, and also wedding and christening cakes, fruit loaves, barn bracks (a kind of currant bun), sally lunns (sweet tea cakes), wine loaves and sugar cake. Although increased traffic and the central reservation have changed the roadway over the years, the street retains much of its original character.

Arriving from Belfast where he served his time as a butcher, twenty-two year old Matthew Alexander Quail set up shop in Rathfriland Street in 1897. He is pictured here with his wife Dora and their first daughter, Lily, who was born in 1900. Not long after this the business moved to 15 Newry Street where it is still going strong. Expansion saw the acquisition of a shop in Dromore and also the creation the partnership of Kirker & Quail to haul coal to Seapatrick mill. One of the first cars in Banbridge was Matthew's Armstrong Siddeley. Lily was joined by seven brothers and sisters and went on to marry Robert Curran who worked as a butcher with her father. Matthew died in 1930, aged fifty-four years, and Dora died in 1951. Matthew's son, Joseph, ran the business from 1930 until 1979, when he retired and passed it on to his sons.

The Walsh brothers, one of whom was called David, outside their shop at 30 Newry Street in the early 1900s. Although they were chiefly ironmongers, they also sold house furnishings, boots and leather merchandise, and, as agricultural suppliers to the farming community around Banbridge, milk churns and ploughs. Above the shop, David's wife ran the Commercial Hotel which catered for commercial travellers. Following the deaths of the Walshs, Robert Martin bought the business in 1940 and moved the shop across to 67 Newry Street in 1969.

The Downshire Arms Hotel in 1902 (the name given on the card is an error). One of the two ladies here may have been Mrs Chambers, the then proprietress. This building dates from 1816. In 1804 its predecessor, also a hostelry, was assessed by the architect Robert Sharland as being ' . . . in a most wretched condition, the roof ready to fall, the offices nearly down, the barn and most of the outhouses proped [sic] . . . ' One of Mrs Chambers' daughters was a doctor who used the lower right-hand apartment as a surgery. Excepting the loss of a chimney and the addition of a satellite dish, the building is little changed.

Newry Road, running into Newry Street and the Downshire Bridge, pictured from the Fort Street junction in the early twentieth century. On the left stands the tollhouse (since demolished) with the terrace of Mount Royal behind. Just coming into view is one of the vans which belonged to Patterson, the Belfast baker.

The lower end of Bridge Street, with a horse and trap outside Young & Co., the draper's premises on the left. Mr Joseph Young, a local councillor and JP, was the last family member in the business which closed in the 1960s. The lettering of 'Arcade' survives and the shop is now occupied by the second-hand shop, Just As New.

Prominent in this 1912 view of Bridge Street rising towards the Downshire Bridge are the poplar trees, planted on each side of the Cut in 1879, six years before the opening of the present bridge. The stone for the bridge, a hard granite, came from Lisnaree. On the far right of the picture is T. & A. Wallace the grocers, who traded until the late 1950s.

Bridge Street looking towards the bridge with the old RUC barracks and the spire of Seapatrick Church (built 1837) in the centre of the view. One of the few shops identifiable in this photograph (on the right) is the 'Wireless shop' of P.E. Neeson, the electrical contractor who was based at 63 Bridge Street.

The Picture House Café on Bridge Street in the 1920s. Posing with an assistant is Joe Beck, an usher in the adjoining Picture House, who stayed at 41 Rathfriland Street with his wife and son, Derek. The Bacci family rented the café from J.U. Finney, the owner of the cinema, until September 1938 when Bernard Scappiaticci and family from Belfast took over and renamed it the Bridge Café (Bernard died in 1951). For a time in the early 1980s it was the 'Boutique' and is now the premises of S. Sawyers & Co., estate agents. The cinema, which had opened in 1912, closed in 1956.

This photograph of Hale's 'New Premises' in Bridge Street probably dates from 1895 when the business was opened. Despite this display of poultry and sides of beef, he traded on the slogan 'bacon is the backbone of our business'. Remembered in his later years as 'a peppery old fellow', Richard (Dick) J. Hale, pictured here on the left, lived at Huntley House.

Built in the 1860s as an office for the Downshire Estates and later taken as the barracks for the Royal Irish Constabulary, the Ulster Architectural Heritage Society's survey describes this yellow brick-dressed, blackstone edifice as 'dour, but full of character, rather like a policeman's uniform'. Pictured here in 1904, it has changed little but has been empty and abandoned since the police moved to their new barracks in Castlewellan Road in January 1991. These took the site of Cantrell & Cochrane, the mineral water bottlers.

The Masonic Hall in Church Square, 1904. Built by the Presbyterian Non-Subscribing Church and opened on 6 October 1844, it served them until congregational divisions in the mid-1880s. In 1893 it was bought by Lodge 336 of the Masonic Order for £390 and was dedicated on 4 October 1898. The lodge had previously met in members' homes. Since this photograph was taken, rooms have been added to the left side and the urns on the roofline have been removed. However, the lion still sits at the front gable apex – although no-one can now explain why it is there. This image was taken by a local photographer, William John Napier, who travelled the countryside in a horse and trap. After his death in May 1914, he was laid to rest at Tanderagee Presbyterian Churchyard alongside his leg which had been amputated and buried there ten years earlier.

Church Square in the early twentieth century when it was uncluttered by central reservations, lane markings, traffic lights, bollards and road signs. Dromore Street and Hill Street stretch into the distance while on the left stand the Masonic Hall and Seapatrick Parish Church (then surrounded by trees). In the centre of the square is the Crozier Monument. Designed by W.J. Barre of Newry and erected in 1862 at a cost of £700, it commemorates Captain Francis Rawdon Moira Crozier (1796–1848) who died in the frozen wastes of Canada while serving with the Franklin Expedition which was seeking the North-West Passage.

Built in 1791 by George Crozier, a Banbridge solicitor and father of Captain Francis Crozier, the three-storey Crozier House dominates Church Square. Realising its historic importance, it was bought in 1968 by Mr Lloyd Cowdy and extensive restoration work was carried out.

Church Square viewed from the Castlewellan Road junction and looking towards Dromore Street, *c.*1912. Hanna Hillen, financial consultants, now occupy the first two-storey house, while beyond Crozier House conversions have created the Coach Inn lounge and restaurant. Flanagan the undertaker's is now the Jockey Club. The United Co-operative Baking Society's van, which distributed the Society's Belfast-baked bread around Banbridge, was operated by their local agent, Samuel Cruikshank.

Church Street, looking out towards Lurgan Road in 1911. This once quiet residential terrace was built before 1850, along with Riversley House, the gate of which is on the right. Today the trees are gone, many of the houses are offices, and standing on the roadway would be a lot more dangerous.

Born in Scarva Street on Hallowe'en 1852, James White married twenty-eight year old Jane Fryar of Yellowhill in June 1887 and emigrated to Chicago, Illinois. By 1896 they had five children and James later became proprietor of the James White Paper Company of Chicago. Following his death in April 1919, the family donated a set of ten bells, cast by the bellfounder John Taylor of Loughborough, to Seapatrick Parish Church. In White's memory they play 'Home Sweet Home' every Hallowe'en.

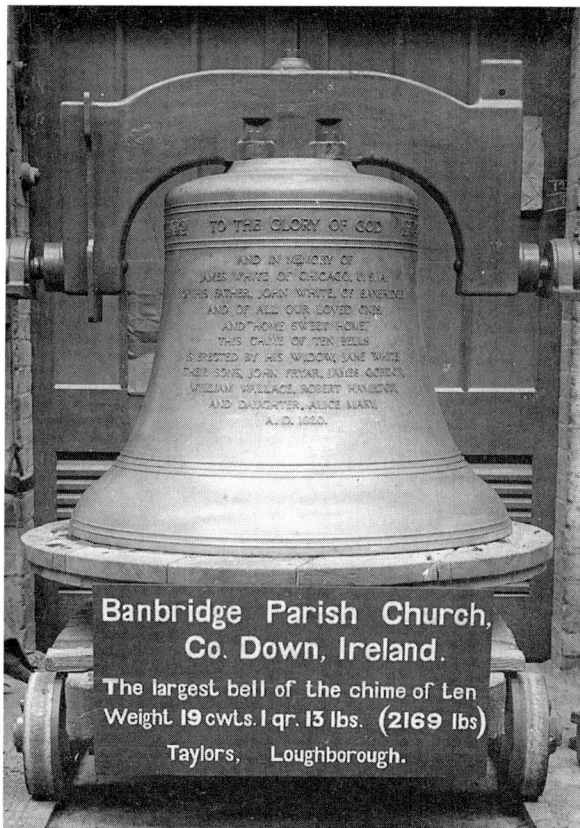

Banbridge Parish Church, Co. Down, Ireland.
The largest bell of the chime of ten
Weight 19 cwts. 1 qr. 13 lbs. (2169 lbs)
Taylors, Loughborough.

Right: The Brownies of Seapatrick Church at their annual inspection in the church grounds – where the church hall now stands – in the early 1930s. First in the line is Lily Anderson and third along stands Sadie Gault. In front of the rank is Sadie McDowell who would later be instrumental in setting up the Banbridge Trefoil Guild – the 'Granny Guides' – in February 1952 (the Guild's inaugural meeting opened with a two minutes silence for the death King George VI). The inspection of the Brownies was taken by May Martin, Dr Martin's daughter who later became Mrs Ervin and moved to Devon. A stained-glass window in the church reads, 'To the Glory of God and in Loving Memory of Rosaleen Knight (neé Kerr) who founded the Girl Guides in Banbridge in 1924. The gift of the Trefoil Guild, her family and friends.'

The 1st Banbridge Brownies, and friends, pose in front of a Belfast Omnibus Company's bus in Church Square before setting off on their annual outing – probably to somewhere on the coast – around 1936. Of the two little girls in white in the centre of the row, the one on the left is Jean Harper.

Barely recognisable today, this is Lancasterian School off Church Street, with its vegetable garden (now a parking area) sweeping down to the river. The row of cottages to the right was owned by Ferguson's mill. Established in 1829, the school was named after Joseph Lancaster (1778–1838), or more correctly his 'monitorial' system of education, for it is doubtful if he ever set foot in Ireland. Born of a Quaker family in Southwark, London, he pioneered the 'mass schooling' of poorer children, and through necessity and lack of staff developed a system of class supervision by monitors, i.e. the older and brighter pupils taught the younger ones. Probably set up in Banbridge by the Royal Lancasterian Society, the earliest known teachers here were husband and wife Adam and Hester Glass who had a role of 141 pupils. The school survived until the early 1950s, when the trustees began letting it to local organisations, including the Scouts, the Angling Club and pigeon fanciers. Years of neglect took their toll and in 1985 it was sold and converted to five flats (known as Lancasterian Court), with the new houses of Weavers Court built around it.

Dromore Street in 1914, when this picture was taken, was a mixture of housing and business. The street was the site of Wright's Garage, opened by that family after they had given up Lenaderg Post Office, and D. McConville & Sons, the poultry and egg exporters, who used to advertise for the following: 'Wanted, any quantity of old hens and all classes of poultry'. The street went through many years of stagnation until 1975 when much of it was demolished to make way for neo-Georgian houses put up by the Housing Executive.

The Rev. John Rooney, with trowel in hand, lays the foundation stone of St Patrick's Hall, Hill Street, in the winter of 1914. The building was completed the following year. The Rev. Rooney had been appointed to Banbridge on 30 October 1907, upon his return from America where he had been raising funds for Newry Cathedral since 1904. Over the years the hall has held many meetings and innumerable dances and whist drives.

Banbridge Railway Station in the 1950s. In the earlier part of its ninety-eight years of operation, its most important role was in the transport of finished linen products. The station closed in the April 1956.

Drum Major Bob Mills leads the Banbridge Silver Band along Eden Terrace on Victoria Street in the 1930s. Founded as Banbridge Amateur Brass Band at a meeting in the Temperance Hall on 22 August 1892, Harry Gill was appointed chairman and conductor. In the late 1940s they changed to silver instruments and in 1951 purchased navy blue and red trimmed uniforms. A change of uniform occurred again in the mid-1980s when they adopted maroon jackets and black trousers with maroon trim.

Rockview Football Club, which drew its players from the Dromore Street area, pictured during the 1910–11 season. This was one of many Banbridge teams which played on Murray's Meadow on Bannview Terrace. It has not been possible to name the players, but on the left stands William Close, with James Carson on the right. William's devotion to football, as player and referee, was lifelong and he was also involved with Banbridge Town F.C. He died in 1970 at eighty years of age. Jim Carson, on the other hand, lived a short life. At the outbreak of the Great War he joined the Royal Irish Rifles and on Wednesday, 28 June 1916, was killed by a shell while marching to the front for the opening of the Battle of the Somme. Aged thirty years, he left a widow, Mary, and a two year old son. He lies in Martinsart British Cemetery on the Somme.

Built by John Thompson of Donegall Pass, Belfast, to a design by the County Surveyor, Henry Smyth, the Gothic–Italian style courthouse in Victoria Street cost £2,465 to construct and was opened on 18 October 1874. The courtroom, with its 48 foot high ceiling, takes up the centre portion of the building, while to the left are rooms for lawyers and police, and to the right the magistrates' room and clerk's office. On its centenary dry rot necessitated its closure, and while the £74,000 refurbishment work was carried out, court business took place in the adjacent Orange Hall and the Masonic Hall in Church Square. The court reopened in November 1974.

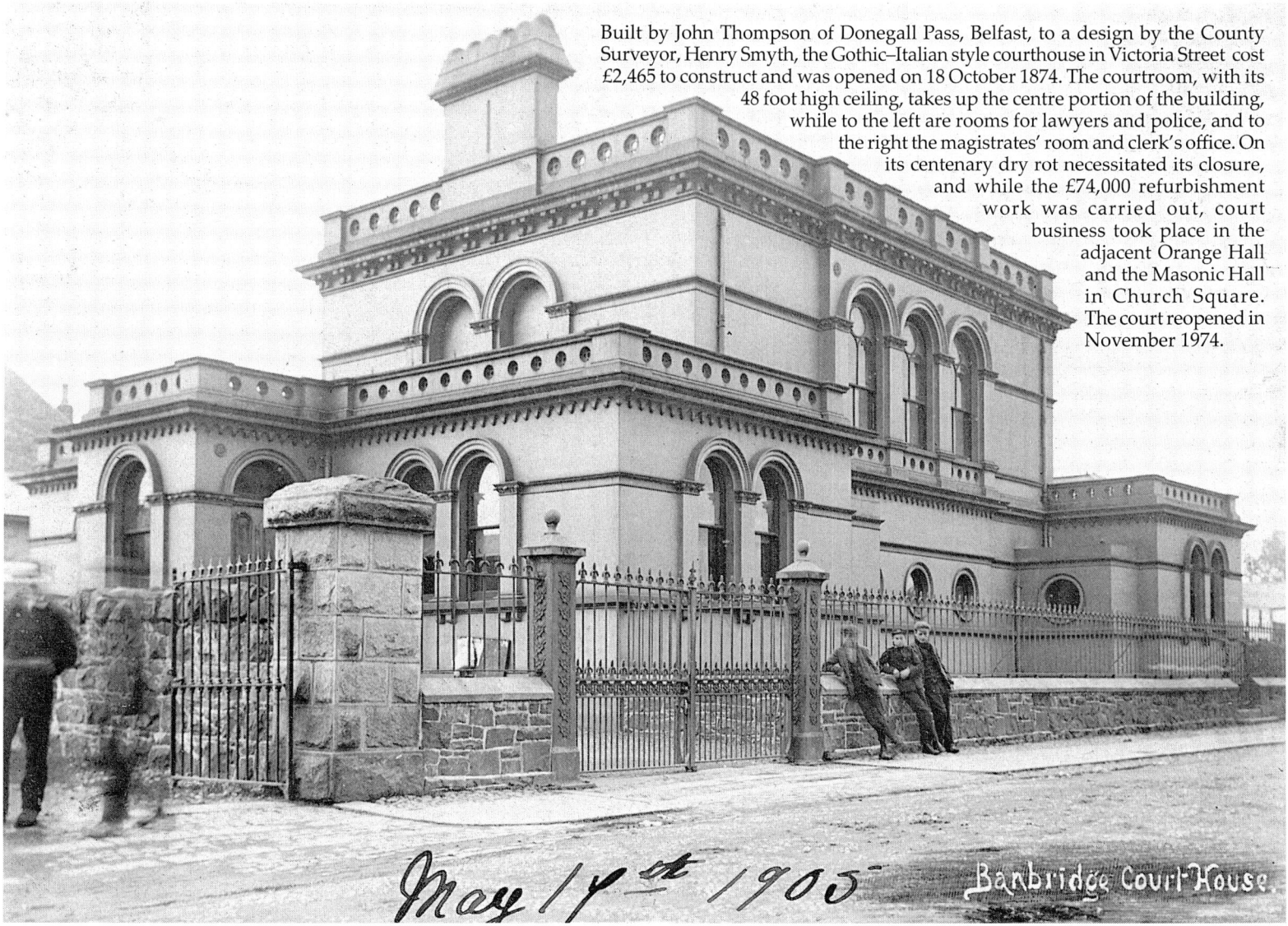

May 14th 1905

Banbridge Court House.

Members of the Mount Nebo Royal Black Preceptory No. 53 (this is a sister organisation of the Orange Order), photographed outside Banbridge Orange Hall in Victoria Street where they still meet today. Opened on 27 May 1882, the two-storey hall originally had four lodge rooms on the ground floor and one on the upper. However, a bomb explosion at the adjacent courthouse in April 1991 so damaged the hall's frontage that it was demolished. The present hall was officially opened on the same site by Brother George Patton, Executive Officer of the Grand Orange Lodge of Ireland, on 25 April 1998.

The now disbanded Orange Hill Union and Crown Defenders, LOL 25, march down Bridge Street in the early 1900s. Their banner honours Brother James McMeekin who had been their Worshipful Master in 1897. Although modernised, the buildings behind the marchers, on the west side of Bridge Street, have changed little.

Accompanied by the Banbridge Conservative Flute Band, a popular band until it folded in 1935, the Sir Knights, a preceptory in Banbridge Black District, march to the railway station on their way to a 13 July celebration, possibly at Scarva, in 1913. Behind the railway wagons stands the Downshire Road Unitarian Church.

This photograph of Reilly Street from around 1910 was typical of the times, as was the housing. The reason for the Salvation Army choosing Reilly Street for their citadel was not without reason as they did much work in this area. Not until the late 1960s was it all swept away and replaced with modern housing. Residents will remember the recently closed Iveagh Cinema which stood just off the lower end of the street.

Founded in London by William Booth in 1865, the Salvation Army, with its quasi-military uniforms and command structure, came to Ireland in 1880, initially basing itself in Belfast, Dublin, Londonderry, Cork and Dunleary. Inaugurated in Banbridge on 4 October 1884, it was 1932 before their Reilly Street Citadel, at the Victoria Street corner, was opened. It is not known where this photograph from the 1920s was taken, but it is said to show: *front row* (left to right): Eddie Pentland and Thomas Shaw; *middle row:* Tommy Lyttle, Jim Shaw, Bill Harrison, Mrs Harrison, Lilian Shaw, and Jim Redpath; *back row*: Jim McBurney, Tom Adair, Joseph Sergison, Jack Stevenson, John Adair and Robert Clydesdale. Although they are recalled for their Saturday night sermons on the Downshire Bridge and their Sunday afternoon marches around the Hill Street and Dromore Street areas, they are best remembered for their member Bessie Whiteside, who trailed the pubs on a Saturday night with a song and copies of the journal *War Cry*.

Opened on 11 January 1933 by the Duchess of Abercorn and Lord Craigavon, the ninety-three bed Banbridge District Hospital was furnished with the latest technology of the time, including an X-ray suite. The local newspaper even boasted that every patient had 1,250 cubic feet of air space! The hospital took the site of the old workhouse which had been built in 1841 when there was need for such an institution to house the very poor of the town. With its piecemeal extensions, this could accommodate 800. By the end of the nineteenth century it was needed more as a hospital as the sick slowly replaced the depleting numbers of the needy, but it retained the workhouse stigma. Eventually the need for a modern hospital was recognised and in 1932 the workhouse was demolished. Closure for the District Hospital came in December 1996 when services were transferred to Craigavon Area Hospital.

The Downshire Bridge and Newry Street decorated with flags and bunting for the visit of Sir Edward Carson on Thursday, 18 September 1913. Carson was a Dublin MP and lawyer (he successfully represented the Marquis of Queensbury in his case against Oscar Wilde) who in 1910 became leader of the Irish Unionist Party and as such was a key opponent of home rule. On the back of this photograph are written the names Jim Newell, Alex Hall, W. Ryan, W. Hoey, P. Turley and D. Gamble; presumably these were the boys pictured.

Carson's visit attracted 25,000 people from the countryside around Banbridge, some of whom are pictured here awaiting his arrival. The council declared the day of the visit a general holiday, as can be observed by the drawn blinds and closed gate of the Dickson Bros.' drapery shop. Dicksons', where 'dress and mantle making is done on the premises by a First-Class scientific dress cutter', was bought over by McMurray in 1920.

The first of the motorcade bringing Carson from Newry follows the Ulster Volunteer Force men of Gilford, Waringstown, Loughbrickland and Banbridge up Bridge Street. The men had mustered at Market Yard in Victoria Street and, headed by the Conservative Flute Band and the Banbridge Brass Band, marched to Dromore Street where they were joined by the visitors. Later they massed in the grounds of Belmont House for an inspection by Carson before he went on to Dromore.

Carson made an address from Bridge Street and after he had left the crowds started to disperse. On a postcard dated 30 September 1913, the sender wrote, 'We had a great day here last Thursday week. Sir E. Carson was here'. He returned to Banbridge in May 1914 when, at a ceremony at Lenaderg, he presented the Ulster Volunteer Force with the colours which are now in Seapatrick Church.

Nurses of the Ulster Volunteer Force, photographed walking down from Seapatrick to Currie's Turn, also took part in the parade. At the time they were based at Edenderry House and during the Great War they tended wounded men at Dunbarton House in Gilford. On the Monday following Carson's visit the Picture House was able to show a 'full pictorial record of the procession and inspection'.

For many years Ballievey Suspension Bridge carried traffic over the River Bann until advancing age brought a weight restriction of 10 tons (later reduced to 5 tons). This worked well enough until September 1988, when the driver of a bulk tanker heading for the bleach works did not see the sign among the branches and, with most of the bridge, ended up in the Bann. The remnants of the old bridge were removed and its successor opened to traffic on 1 September 1989.

Thomas Ferguson established this linen mill on the river bank in the 1850s. Initially powered by water, it soon converted to steam-driven looms and another chimney rose on the Banbridge skyline.

The 'English-style' houses at Hayes Park, Seapatrick, were built by the owners of Hayes' Mill for their employees. In their day they carried status: while workers were housed in the rows of cottages behind, these new houses were for the foremen. The rural setting was initially emphasised by the absence of both roads and footpaths; the development was said to be 'Hayes by name and a maze by nature'.

Opened by Hayes' Mill around 1900, Seapatrick Co-operative shop on Lurgan Road, at its corner with Tonaghmore Road, traded until the late 1960s by which time it was a 'supermarket' type shop. In the early years the upper floor contained a grain and flour store, while through the double doors on the left was the coal yard. The building has passed through many hands over the years, but has been the premises of Mill Court Antiques since 1995.

This photograph from 1913 shows the Old Parish Church, Seapatrick, when its lonely gable wall was ivy covered. The church dated from 1698 and due to the expansion of Banbridge it was replaced by Seapatrick Parish Church in Church Square in the early nineteenth century. The old church was bought by the Hayes family in 1847 and they had its stones used to build the perimeter wall of the graveyard, leaving only the gable. Tradition has it that the church was founded by St Patrick who rested by a well, or spring, on the site. The name Seapatrick derives from *Sui Phadraig* or 'St Patrick's resting place'. The old fellow in the photograph cannot be identified. He may simply have posed at random, or he may have been connected with the stone in front of him which was erected in 1860 by Robert Flanagan to the memory of his children, John, Joseph, John, Samuel, Mary and Robert. Was the old man a surviving child or could he have been Flanagan himself?

The post office and store at Lenaderg, 'the place of the red soil', in 1914. At that time it was run by the Wright family who moved on to found Wright's Engineering Garage in Dromore Street, Banbridge, in 1921. Standing in the centre is Dick Wright, flanked by two of his sons, possibly Simpson and Richard. The business goes back to the 1840s (a letter franked here in 1848 survives) when it was opened as a co-operative by the mill owners Wm. Smyth & Co. The need for a post office stemmed from the fact that mill workers were drawn from all over the country. The Wrights were succeeded by Herbert James Martin (his name is still above the door) who came from a grocer's shop in Lawrencetown. Herbert died in 1927, leaving his widow Sadie and his sons Roy and Billy to run the business. The hours were long – the post office opened at 8.00 a.m. and closed at 7.30 p.m., while the shop stayed open until 8.00 p.m. and 10.00 p.m. on Fridays and Saturdays. In April 2000 the post office side was relinquished, leaving Roy to concentrate on the provisions side.

William Smyth & Co.'s bleaching fields and mill at Lenaderg. Running across the foreground is the Banbridge to Scarva railway line, with Lenaderg Station which closed in 1955. There was also a siding into the works, although this closed in 1929.

A horse-drawn wagon brings in bleached linen to Smyth & Co.'s mill at Lenaderg. It is thought that William Kerr is driving the horse. The works closed down just prior to the Second World War and were eventually demolished. In the spring of 2002 work started on a new housing estate on the site to be named Linen Fields.